Dear Parent:

Do you want to spark your child's creativity? Do you want your child to become a confident writer? Road to Writing can help.

Road to Writing is a unique creative writing program that gives even the youngest writers a chance to express themselves. Featuring five distinct levels, or Miles, the Road to Writing program accompanies children from their first attempts at writing to comfortably writing on their own.

A Creative Start
For children who "write" stories by drawing pictures
• easy picture prompts • familiar subjects • places to draw

Creative Writing With Help
For children who write easy words with help
• detailed picture prompts • places to draw and label

Creative Writing On Your Own
For children who write simple sentences on their own
• basic story starters • popular topics • places to write

First Journals
For children who are comfortable writing short paragraphs
• more complex story starters • space for free writing

Journals
For children who want to try different kinds of writing
• cues for poems, jokes, stories • brainstorming pages

There's no need to hurry through the Miles. Road to Writing is designed without age or grade levels. Children can progress at their own speed, developing confidence and pride in their writing ability along the way.

Road to Writing—"write" from the start!

Look for these
Road to Writing
books

Mile 1

Animal Crackers
Cool School
Mostly Monsters
Super Me!

Mile 2

Boo!
Dinosaur Days
Get a Clue!
Road Trip

Mile 3

Barbie: Always in Style
Happily Never After: Tangled Tales
Monkey Business
Sports Shorts

Tips for Using this Book

- Help your child read each page. Then let your child draw or write a response—right in the book!

- Don't worry—there are no "right" or "wrong" answers. This book is a place for your child to be creative.

- Remind your child to write at his or her own pace. There's no rush!

- Encourage your child with plenty of praise.

Pencils, pens, and crayons are all suitable for use in this book. Markers are not recommended.

A GOLDEN BOOK • New York
Golden Books Publishing Company, Inc. New York, New York 10106

ISBN: 0-307-45410-X   A MMI

Dinosaur Days

by Michelle Knudsen and

_____
(your name)

illustrated by Dave Garbot and

_____
(your name)

Your Great Aunt Sally sent you a pet dinosaur for your birthday.

Draw what it looks like.

My dinosaur's name

is _____.

What does your dinosaur eat?
Pick one, or make up your own.

Pizza

Lima Beans

Flowers

Mud

Ice Cream _____

Draw a picture of your family eating dinner.

(Don't forget your pet dinosaur!)

Your dinosaur is too big to live in your house.

Create a new home for your dinosaur.

Write words that describe it.

_____   _____

_____   _____

_____   _____

_____   _____

Draw it.

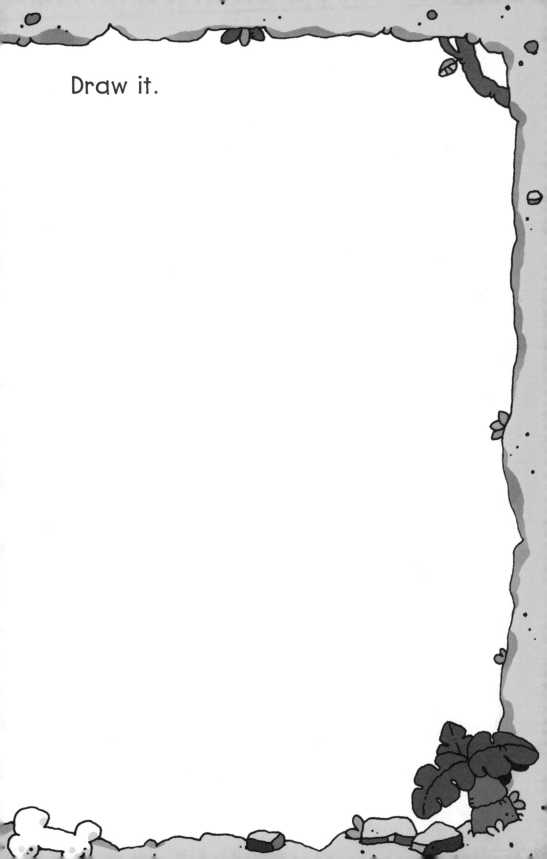

Oh, no! Your pet dinosaur is lost.
Make up a sign to put
in your neighborhood.

LOST DINOSAUR

Goes by the name: _____

Color: _____

Height: _____ feet

Last seen at: _____

If found, please call: _____

Draw a sketch of your dinosaur for the sign.

Phew! Your pet dinosaur has been found.

Write a thank-you note to the person who found your dinosaur.

Dear _____,

Thank you for returning

_____ to me.

I am _____ to have my

dinosaur back.

Sincerely,

_____

Draw a picture of you and the person who found your dinosaur.

Teach your pet dinosaur
a new trick.

Draw the different steps.

Roll over.

DINO TREATS

Step 1

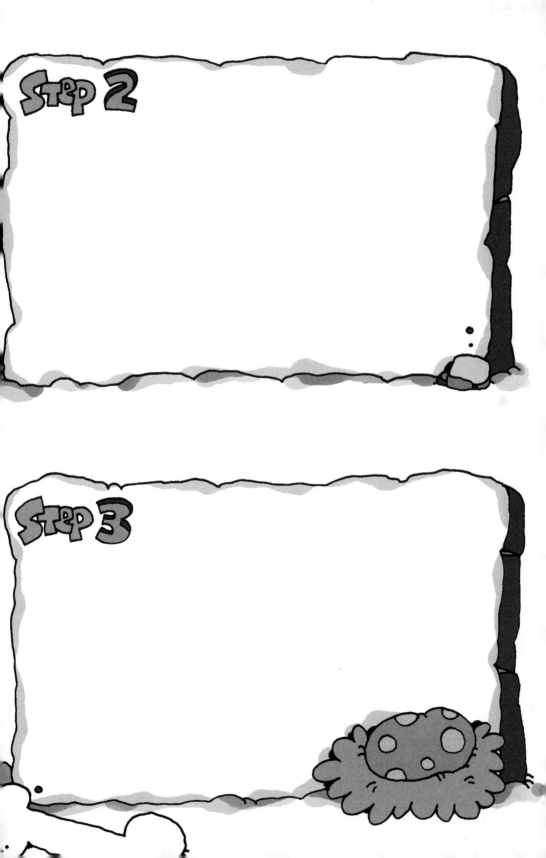

You have designed a new pair of shoes for your dinosaur.

Draw a picture of the shoes.

What makes these shoes special?

Your dinosaur has the flu.
Make a get-well card.

Draw the picture here.

Fill in the message.

Dear _____,

I hope you _____

_____.

Make sure to _____

_____.

Love,

_____

Things I like about having a pet dinosaur:

(Check which ones.)

_____ Someone to play catch with

_____ Always have a ride to school

What else?

_____

_____

_____

Things I DON'T like about having a pet dinosaur:

a pet dinosaur:

(Check which ones.)

_____ Cleaning up
after it

_____ Sharing my
room

What else?

_____

_____

_____

While taking your dinosaur
for a walk, you found these
footprints.

Draw a picture of the dinosaur
you think made them.

Name the dinosaur:

_____

You are throwing a birthday party for your pet dinosaur.

Fill out the invitation.

Birthday Party

For: _____

Date: _____

Time: _____

Place: _____

Draw the pictures you took
at the party.

You and your pet dinosaur are going to visit your Great Aunt Sally.

What will you need to pack?

My packing list:

_____   _____

_____   _____

_____   _____

Draw everything in your suitcase.

My pet dinosaur's packing list:

_____   _____

_____   _____

_____   _____

Draw everything in your dinosaur's suitcase.

Send your parents
a postcard from your trip.

Draw the picture.

Fill in the message.

Dear Mom and Dad,
The weather is

_____.

Today, we are going

to _____.

See you soon!

Love,

_____

Postage
2Rocks

You entered your dinosaur
in a pet show.

Draw the dinosaur that won
each prize.

Make up your own prize.

You brought your pet dinosaur to school for show-and-tell.

What did the other kids bring?

Your new pen pal
has a pet dinosaur, too.
Write a letter to your new pen pal.

Dear _____,

My name is _____.

My pet dinosaur's name is

_____.

Our favorite thing to do is

_____.

I hope we can meet soon!

From,

_____
(your name)

Draw a picture of your
pen pal's dinosaur.

While digging for bones in your backyard, your pet dinosaur discovered a hidden treasure chest.

Write down the things you found in it.

_____

_____

_____

_____

_____

_____

Draw them.

Your dinosaur is going to pet school.

What will your dinosaur learn to do?

1. _____

2. _____

3. _____

Draw a picture of one of the things.

What will your dinosaur
learn NOT to do?

1._____

2._____

3._____

Draw a picture of one of the things.

You and your dinosaur
have entered a talent show.

What will you and your dinosaur
do in the show?

_____

_____

_____

What will you and your dinosaur
wear?

_____

_____

_____

Draw a picture of you and your dinosaur in the talent show.

You and your dinosaur
won first place in
the talent show.

What is the prize?

_____

_____

Draw it!

Draw you and your
dinosaur on the
six o'clock news.

Our Scrapbook

_____ and
(your name)

_____
(your pet dinosaur's name)

Finish the captions.
Then draw the pictures.

A day at the _____

Lunch at _____

A weekend at _____

Draw a picture of what
you and your pet dinosaur
will look like in ten years.

and Me